GW00786480

Take up
Swimming

Take up Swimming

Principal contributors:
Paul Bush
Swimming Development Officer, City of Leeds
Terry Denison
Chief Swimming Coach, City of Leeds
Chief Coach to the British Swimming Team

SPRINGFIELD BOOKS LIMITED

Copyright © Springfield Books Limited and White Line Press
1989

ISBN 0 947655 70 0

First published 1989 by
Springfield Books Limited
Springfield House, Norman Road, Denby Dale, Huddersfield
HD8 8TH

Edited, designed and produced by
White Line Press
60 Bradford Road, Stanningley, Leeds LS28 6EF

Edited: Noel Whittall and Philip Gardner
Design: Krystyna Hewitt
Diagrams: Steve Beaumont, Barry Davies

Printed and bound in Great Britain

This book is copyright under the Berne Convention. All rights
are reserved. Apart from any fair dealing for the purposes of
private study, research, criticism or review, as permitted
under the Copyright Act, 1956, no part of this publication
may be reproduced, stored in a retrieval system, or trans-
mitted in any form or by any means, electronic, electrical,
chemical, mechanical, optical, photocopying, recording or
otherwise, without the prior written permission of the
copyright owner. Enquiries should be addressed to the
Publishers.

Photographic credits

Cover photograph: Sporting Pictures (UK) Limited
Sid Greaves: pages 32, 33 (top)
Speedo: page 11
Swimming Times: pages 37, 44
All other photographs by Noel Whittall

Contents

Introduction

Welcome to swimming! You have chosen a sport which will provide lots of fun, keep you fit, and may one day allow you to save your own life or that of someone else.

Most people manage to learn to swim after a fashion. This book will show you how to swim *well*. You will learn to perform the strokes efficiently, and how to master the all-important matter of timing. As your skill increases, you may well find that you would like to join a club and take up competitive swimming. If your basic technique is correct, you will find that your progress in the sport will be rapid.

Swimming is a very easy sport to get into: the equipment you need is minimal, and most towns have one or more public swimming pools. If you learn to swim at a pool in one of the many official pro- grammes or award schemes (see pages 34–35 for further details), you can be sure that you will also learn the essentials of water safety.

We recommend that you only swim in purpose-built swimming pools until you are very experienced: the dangers of running water (rivers) or tidal water (estuaries or the open sea) are obvious, and lakes and ponds can be full of dangerous underwater hazards.

Safety in swimming

There are dangers in swimming, but if you respect the dangers and keep to a set of simple rules, your swimming will be safe and enjoyable.

Remember:

- Don't swim immediately after a meal, as this may cause dangerous stomach cramps
- Never swim alone
- Never dive into dark water or shallow pools
- Never swim in cold open water — you run out of energy amazingly quickly
- Don't go out of your depth until you are a really competent swimmer
- Treat the sea with the greatest respect: understand how easy it is to stray out of your depth

1

For non-swimmers

If you *want* to swim, you can learn to swim. *Everybody* can learn to swim; it is almost impossible to be too old or too young. A book can help you, but the only place to really learn is in the water.

Babies and toddlers

Youngsters can be taken to the pool as early in life as you wish. Many parents feel that six months is the right age for their children to start, and some local authorities run special "Mother and Baby" classes which are very popular. The object at this early age is simply to familiarise the baby with the water. Whether you go to a class, or just take your baby to the normal sessions, you should hold the child all the time it is in the water, allowing it to splash and enjoy itself as much as it wants. Don't frighten the child by moving around the pool too rapidly — a slow walk is quite fast enough. It is important that the water is comfortably warm — don't let the infant become chilled.

The impression a child gets when first introduced to the water can stay to the end of its life, so make sure that these early experiences are totally pleasant.

Young children

A pair of inflated arm bands can help youngsters to develop confidence early on. In formal lessons these will usually be provided by the pool authority, and their use will be supervised. However, if your children are to use their own arm bands, you must take extra care: remember that arm bands are swimming aids, not life protectors. Supervise carefully any young children wearing arm bands, and do not allow them to drift unattended into deep water.

The best early advice anyone can have is not to be afraid of putting their face in the water. You can't learn to swim and keep your face dry, so get used to getting it soaked early on! Some children are very nervous about this, and they must be encouraged to overcome their fears, but never *forced* to overcome them.

A good method is to get the child to blow into the water – first from just above the surface, then with the lips touching it, and finally with the mouth right under the water. Variations on this sort of game are usually successful if the child is not subjected to too much pressure. The knack of blowing air out of the mouth when underwater will become useful later, when the breast stroke, butterfly or crawl strokes are being learned.

Lessons can be started at virtually any age. We advise you to seek professional help at this stage and pass your youngster over to a qualified instructor at the earliest opportunity. With very young children, Mum or Dad will still be needed to help with dressing and undressing and to provide quiet but cheerful encouragement. *Be patient*: children develop at different rates in all aspects of life – including learning to swim. Be tolerant with your son or daughter, and keep

smiling. Learning to swim can be a daunting experience for some young people and they need constant encouragement and reassurance. *They will almost all swim in their own good time.*

Awards schemes

Courses of lessons are often linked to an awards scheme, so that progress can be marked by badges and diplomas. Most young swimmers who take formal swimming lessons follow the awards path and then move on into a swimming training scheme or local club. Details of the most popular British schemes appear on pages 34–35.

Adult learners

Do go to one of the many classes which are organised especially for adults learning to swim. Get wet all over! Enjoy the sessions; try hard, but don't take it all desperately seriously; after a very few sessions, you will be swimming — it really is as simple as that.

If you are nervous in the water, build up your confidence in exactly the same way as suggested for children. Once you have overcome your fear of having your face in the water, you will be able to "glide" in waist-deep water by pushing yourself forwards and allowing your feet to come off the bottom. By adding leg kicks and simple arm strokes, you will soon be able to prolong the glide for as long as you can comfortably hold your breath.

When you can make your strokes smooth and powerful enough to raise your mouth above the water at regular intervals, you are on the way to mastering the art of swimming.

No matter how old you are, you will almost certainly find that learning to swim is more fun and easier if you are with a friend or small group.

2

Swimming for sport

Equipment

Very little equipment is needed to begin a successful swimming programme. All that is essential is a good towel and a pair of trunks or a swim suit. We recommend that caps are worn by everyone, and indeed some pool authorities insist on them to reduce the amounts of hair and grease in the water.

Goggles are a matter of personal choice. If you decide that your swimming would be more pleasant when wearing them, then get a good-quality pair which will keep the water out without having to be excessively tight.

The strokes

Once you have learned to swim with reasonable confidence, you can begin to think about improving your style. So far you have been concerned simply with staying afloat and making any sort of progress; developing style will automatically mean that you will move through the water faster and with far less effort than before. There are four basic strokes in competitive swimming: *breast stroke*, *back stroke*, *front crawl* and *butterfly*. The action of each is defined by laws laid down by FINA, the world governing body of swimming. They are fully defined in *The Laws of the Sport*, published by the Amateur Swimming Association (ASA), but if you follow the advice given here you will not be in danger of developing an "illegal" stroke. We will also cover the basic lifesaving stroke, the *inverted back stroke*.

We describe each stroke by dividing it into five main elements:

- body position
- arm action
- leg action
- breathing
- timing

It will be up to you to put these all together in the water! You can practise the leg action with the aid of a float, or by holding on to the edge of the pool; the arm action can be practised squatting in the water. Get a coach or experienced friend to criticise your stroke.

Using a kick board

3
Breast stroke

Body position

You lie on your stomach in the water, with arms and legs outstretched — we call this the *streamlined position* (Figure 1).

Figure 1

Arm action

From the streamlined position, turn your hands with palms angled outwards, and press your arms outwards, keeping your elbows straight, until they are each at an angle of about forty-five degrees. Now sweep your hands round and in towards your chest in a strong sculling movement. Your hands come together again in front of your chin, and are then extended forward to the streamlined position once more. Throughout the movement, your hands should remain in front of your shoulders.

Figure 2 (continued on next page)

13

Figure 2 (continued)

Leg action

From the streamlined position, bend your knees so that you bring your heels up towards your buttocks; your ankles should be relaxed and slightly apart.

Figure 3

Now turn your feet outwards and make a strong backward movement. When seen from above, each foot should should describe a half-circle, moving outwards and backwards to thrust against the water and so drive the body forward. The kick is completed when the legs and ankles come together in the streamlined position, where they pause for a moment to allow the body to glide forward.

Breathing

You breathe in as your hands sweep in, when your arms are brought round and in towards the chest. This strong movement causes your head and chest to rise, and your mouth will lift far enough out of the water for a breath to be taken in. You must keep your head still, looking straight forward. As your arms extend forward again, your head will naturally descend back into the water, and you should breathe out into the water as you glide forward in the streamlined position.

When the breast stroke is performed correctly, your head comes well above the water and there is plenty of time to take a breath.

Figure 4

Timing

Good timing is the key to an efficient breast stroke. Let's take a look at the full sequence:

1 From the streamlined position, your hands begin to sweep outwards and your head starts to rise upwards. At this stage your legs remain extended behind in the streamlined position.

2 Your arms sweep around and inwards, lifting your head to a position above the surface which allows a breath to be drawn in.

3 As your arms are nearing the completion of their upsweep, you begin to bend your knees to bring your heels up to your buttocks.

4 When your hands begin to extend forward, your legs now sweep round and backwards, so driving your body forward into the streamlined position again.

Common faults in breast stroke

Asymmetric kick (the *screw* kick)
This can be a real problem; the lop-sided kick is inefficient, and can get you disqualified in competition. There are several possible causes, and it can be quite difficult to cure. Check the following:

Cause: Turning the head to one side — particularly during the learning stage.

Cure: Practise holding the glide position absolutely straight and making slow, symmetrical strokes.

Cause: One foot turned out more than the other.

Cure: Go back to basic stroke drills, holding on to the side of the bath if necessary.

Cause: Having one knee in a different kicking position from the other.

Cure: This is the tricky one! Go back to basics, and try the stroke with your knees quite close together, concentrating on getting your feet equally turned outwards when kicking. Gradually open out into a more rounded kick, concentrating on keeping your feet turned out during the power stroke. Don't worry about speed at all at this stage — get the stroke right first.

Head bobbing up and down
Cause: Usually, a fear of water splashing into the mouth when breathing.

Cure: Don't attempt to get your mouth quite so high. Your head should be kept still — the natural lift of your body and shoulders is enough to raise it clear of the water as your hands sweep in together.

This swimmer is tilting her head back too far.

Knees coming too far under the body, causing excessive drag

Cause: You are bending at the hips too much when drawing your heels up to your seat.

Cure: Preserve good streamlining by bending your legs more at the knee, rather than at the hip.

Figure 5

4

Back strokes

Back crawl

The type of back stroke most frequently used is the back crawl.

Body position
In the back crawl, you lie on your back with your legs outstretched and your head "pillowed" on the water.

Figure 6

Arm action
The arm action is a "windmill" movement in which one arm propels while the other recovers. Either arm may begin the movement, and the cycle is as follows: From the side, your arm is raised overhead in a relaxed manner but keeping the elbow straight. The arm continues beyond your head and enters the water, *little finger first*, and about in line with your shoulder — don't reach out sideways. Once the hand is back in the water, there are two distinct parts to the propelling action your arm gives: the first is with the hand in the *catch position*, when you will feel it gaining purchase on the water. Your arm remains straight for this phase, and you *pull* on the water. Then, as the hand gets about level with your shoulder, you should bend

Figure 7

your elbow, bringing your hand close to the body, and complete the action with a strong *pushing* motion towards your feet.

Finish off the stroke by extending the wrist so that your palm faces downwards, and recover overhead in the straight-arm position described at the beginning.

Naturally, you use your arms alternately, so that one is pulling while the other is recovering.

Figure 8

You can get more power into the action if you let your body roll into the stroke, which allows the entry to go deeper into the water. Take care not to let your head roll, though — the head should remain still throughout the stroke.

Leg action

The back crawl leg action is simple: your legs remain close together and move in a flutter movement, with each foot kicking upwards in turn. The kick should be quite shallow and fast enough to maintain good balance and to keep the legs in a position near the surface of the water. The toes should break the surface on each up-beat so that they churn up the water. Your knees should remain under the surface all the time.

The straight arms and powerful leg kicks show clearly during this backstroke race.

Timing and breathing

This is not usually a problem in back crawl. Your arms will naturally maintain a position almost opposite to one another, and the fast leg kick easily fits into this arm cycle. You need to develop a breathing rhythm, and we recommend that beginners practise breathing in each time the left arm, say, passes the head, and breathing out as the right arm passes.

Inverted back stroke

This is not a competitive stroke, but can be very useful because it is the most common lifesaving stroke. Basically, it is the breast stroke leg action performed while in the back stroke position. The arms are kept down by the sides of the body, with the hands either still or sculling (see panel).

Sculling is a movement used to maintain balance. The hands (palms downward) are moved towards and away from the body, at hip level.

You should learn the inverted back stroke because:

- It is relatively easy to do once the breast stroke has been mastered.
- It is an easy relaxing stroke to use if you become tired when swimming.
- It forms the basis for all the towing skills used in lifesaving and survival swimming.

Common faults in back stroke

Head too high, or moving too much

Cause: You are probably afraid of water coming over your face.

Cure: Have faith in the correct body position, with your head "pillowed" on the water. Try to keep your head still throughout the stroke.

"Sitting" in the water

Cause: Letting your hips sink too low.

Cure: Exactly the same as the previous cure!

"Cycling" — letting your knees break the surface

Cause: Incorrect leg action.

Cure: Emphasise the kick with your feet more; think of constantly trying to kick a ball off the surface of the water.

5

Front crawl

This is the fastest stroke of all, and so it is naturally the one chosen for freestyle races. It is also the one most commonly used in training and fitness sessions. The front crawl is the most efficient stroke, because there is almost continuous propulsion throughout the stroke cycle, and because the arms are able to work at their most effective angles.

In essence, the rule for freestyle racing is this: you can use any stroke you like, so long as you do not stand up and walk forward.

Body position
You lie flat on your face, with arms and legs stretched out in front and behind in the streamlined position. Your head should be slightly raised so that you look forward and downwards. This slightly raised position is necessary to ensure that your hips and legs will be below the surface of the water.

Figure 9

The water line will usually strike your head at about the normal hair-line level, high up on the forehead.

Arm action
Your arms work alternately, with one propelling while the other recovers. From the streamlined position, you press down and back with one arm; the elbow should be kept high throughout the movement, so that pressure is exerted backwards, towards the feet.

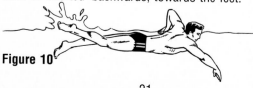

Figure 10

You continue to push with the hand until it is down to the level of your hips. The elbow is then flexed to lift the hand out of the water.

Figure 11

Throughout the recovery your elbow should remain high while the lower arm and hand are carried past the head in a relaxed manner.

It is also important to rotate your body so that your head turns towards the recovering arm in order to take a breath.

As with the back crawl, your arms work alternately, so that one is recovering while the other is propelling.

Leg action

The leg kick is a shallow flutter kick which should churn up the surface behind you. Your legs remain relatively straight, although there will be some knee bending as the feet rise upwards. Each foot kicks downwards in turn, and on the up-beats your heels should just break the surface.

Breathing

In order to keep drag down to a minimum, your head must remain in the water throughout the stroke, with the water level staying at around the hair-line level. This means that you can only breathe when your head is turned to the side.

Competitive swimmers use a number of different breathing patterns, but for the beginner it is best to start by breathing once in each complete arm cycle. You will usually develop a "favourite" side from the beginning, and so will decide to take your breath as the arm on that side is recovering.

Figure 12

Notice how your head pushing through the water creates a bow wave in front of it, followed by a trough; your breath should be taken in this trough.

A freestyle racer about to take a breath in the trough formed by his head pushing through the water

Timing

The timing of the breathing is most important. As explained above, you have to breathe in the trough. To prepare for this breath, you should first breathe out forcibly while your face is right in the water during the earlier part of the stroke. That way you will be ready to take a good breath as soon as your face rocks up into the trough. You should normally be looking along the surface of the water when breathing in. Try to learn to time your breaths really precisely by controlling the amount by which your body rocks, and draw in air exactly as your arm is passing your head on the recovery stroke.

Common faults in front crawl

Excessive head movement

Cause: Lifting your head forward, or turning it too vigorously to breathe.

Cure: Go back to a basic push-and-glide drill: concentrate on holding a good body position, with your head staying in the water; it should turn to the side only just sufficiently for your mouth to clear the surface. Be sure that you have breathed out fully while your face is underwater, so that you are ready to breathe in as soon as your mouth is clear.

"Snaking" — body twisting or wriggling

Cause: This is often due to excessive head movement, or to over-reaching with the hands.

Cure: If head movement is the problem, cure it as described above. If over-reaching is causing the snaking, concentrate on where your hands enter the water: this should be at a point midway between head and shoulder, just a comfortable distance in front of your head. Your hands should enter the water and slide forward into the catch position without stretching, which would pull your hips out of position.

Inefficient hand entry

Cause: Your forearms or elbows enter the water before your hands.

Cure: Keep your elbows high, and make sure that your hand moves cleanly into the catch position.

This beginner is making very good progress during her first attempt to swim butterfly.

6

Butterfly stroke

This is the most demanding of the four strokes, and is usually only taught to swimmers who are fairly competent at the other three strokes. However, butterfly can be exhilarating when swum well, and some young people take to it quickly because they are very supple.

Body position

You remain flat on your chest, with your shoulders level. However, your body will undulate throughout the stroke as shown in Figure 13.

Figure 13

It is this undulation of the body which gives the stroke its appearance of grace and power and gave it its original name, the *butterfly dolphin stroke*.

Arm action

In this stroke both arms work together — the action must be simultaneous and symmetrical. Your hands enter the water at the same time, in front of your head and only about a hand's width apart. You have to keep the elbows up. Now your hands press down to catch the water, and then pull outwards in a similar way to the breast-stroke movement. Next, they sweep in powerfully under your chest before pushing backwards and out, to emerge from the water level with your hips. At the end of the underwater phase you must push your hands out of the water very vigorously so that they will have enough momentum to carry them forward over the water in the recovery phase.

The movement of propulsion is often described as a *keyhole* shape (Figure 14).

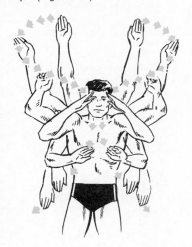

Figure 14

During the recovery of the arms, your head will be out of the water looking forward, and a breath can be taken in. Your arms should sweep forward together, just above the surface of the water, and enter again in front of your head in as relaxed a manner as possible. Try to make your hands enter cleanly, with little splash.

Leg action

Your legs operate together in a strong upward and downward movement. You have to make two leg kicks during each arm cycle. The first kick down should occur as your hands are entering the water; this drives your body down into the stroke and allows your hips to come up into the streamlined position during the pull phase.

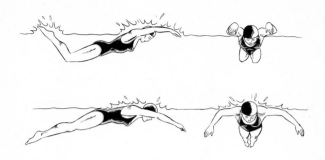

Figure 15

You make the second kick downwards as your hands are leaving the water; this kick carries the body forward while your arms are recovering.

Figure 16

It is important to keep your feet together at all times during the kicking movement. Try to think of them as acting like a dolphin's tail.

Warning — take care when practising the butterfly leg action. Many swimmers use a "kick board" to help them develop their leg action. This is a small float which is held at arm's length while the kick is practised. In the butterfly stroke this can cause problems with the lower back, because it prevents the shoulders and upper body from sinking down into the water as the hips move up. If you feel any discomfort or pain in your back while practising butterfly with a kick board, stop at once.

Breathing

You breathe in when you are looking forward during the recovery of your arms. You won't need to make any special effort to lift your head — it will rise sufficiently because your shoulders are already clearing the water to allow arm recovery.

Figure 17

As your arms pass your ears, your head should be moved forward into the water again. This starts the dive forward into the stroke as the hands re-enter, and in turn helps to raise your hips into the streamlined position.

Timing

Without the correct timing, your butterfly stroke will be inefficient and exhausting. The key is the leg kicks: the first must be made as your hands enter the water; the second as they leave it.

You must also have breathed out under water, so that you are ready to breathe in as soon as your head clears the water when your arms are recovering.

Common faults in butterfly

Body position too flat

Cause: Not letting the body undulate in the "dolphin" manner.

Cure: Start the dolphin action by making sure that your legs kick down and your hips are raised upwards just as your hands enter the water.

Arms "dragging" out of the water

Cause: Failing to push right back and *snap* your arms out of the water. This may be due to lack of strength — butterfly is a very demanding stroke — or it may simply be due to not concentrating enough.

Weak or shallow leg kick

Cause: You're probably keeping your body too flat in the water, or simply not putting enough effort into the kick.

Cure: Concentrate on kicking *down* strongly from your hips. Pay attention to your timing, and remember that there have to be *two* strong kicks in each arm cycle — one as the hands enter the water, and another as they leave it.

7

Racing

The start

For the strokes which are swum on your front, you start with a dive into the water (see page 38). You can gain valuable time by starting fast and diving strongly and efficiently. The idea is for your body to be as streamlined as possible when it enters the water, and at the most efficient angle for the stroke you are going to do. This means that for the crawl you should aim to hit the water at a very shallow angle, as your body lies almost perfectly flat when you are doing the stroke.

The entry for the breast-stroke and butterfly needs to be a little deeper, so always check the pool depth first. As soon as you enter the water, you should arch your back, so that your head surfaces in the correct position to start the stroke.

The competitors in position at the start of a breast-stroke race in a well-organised gala. Costly seconds can be lost by lack of concentration at this point.

Above: *the breaststroke race gets underway*
Below: *swimmers tensed for a backstroke start*

Backstroke races are started with the swimmers in the water, holding on to the edge of the pool. You place your feet quite high up against the side, pulling upwards with your arms, and push powerfully backwards just before the moment of release. You are aiming to get your body high out of the water, arching your back so that your head and arms re-enter first. *Be very careful when you are practising this; don't attempt it in a crowded pool.*

Turning

In races of more than one length, you will have to turn. Learning to do this smoothly and efficiently can save vital seconds. The type of turn you make will be different according to which stroke you are using. In breast-stroke and butterfly, the rules demand that you touch the side of the pool with both hands at the same time, while for backstroke only a one-handed touch is needed. In crawl (freestyle), you are allowed to touch with any part of the body, and so experienced racers use the *flip* or *tumble* turn which is really a form of underwater somersault. In this type of turn, contact with the side of the pool is made with the feet alone.

Breast-stroke and butterfly turn

As your hands touch, you let your body come right up to the side of the pool, drawing your legs up underneath you. Now roll to the side you are going to turn (most right-handers prefer to turn to the left), and you should find that your feet will be nicely positioned to give you a powerful push from the side of the pool. As you push, roll back into the completely face-down position, ready to take up the stroke again as soon as possible.

Freestyle turn

Imagine swimming up to within about two feet (60 cm) from the side, and then bending your head downwards into a perfect somersault; halfway round the somersault, your feet will come into position to push against the pool side, and away you go on a second length. The only problem is that you will be on your back this time if you don't do something about it! The trick is to add a half-twist during the somersault, so that you start the new length in the correct position.

It takes quite a lot of practice to get this sort of turn right. The timing is important, and it is also rather easy to become disoriented during the somersault. It will take many attempts before you can be sure of entering the new length absolutely in line and getting the full benefit of the push.

Gavin Meadows demonstrates the freestyle turn.
Above: *the somersault is completed.*
Top right: *he pushes off powerfully, and begins to roll onto his stomach.*

Backstroke turn

At first, you will simply pull your legs up underneath you as you touch the side of the pool, turn sideways, and then push into the new length. However, you can also do the efficient flip turn in backstroke. This is a little more difficult than when doing it in freestyle. When your hand touches the side, you allow your body to carry on a few inches until your head is close to the wall, then tuck your legs up and drop your head right back. You will flip over rapidly, but would be facing downwards, so you have to include a half-roll to return to the backstroke position. In competition you *must* be on your back when leaving the wall.

The judges are on hand to see a tight finish. At major competitions there are also touch-sensitive pads at the end of the lanes which automatically record the finishing times. ⇒

8
Joining a training scheme

At the time of writing there are nearly 100 swimming training schemes in Great Britain, and new schemes are being added all the time. These all offer full-time professional coaching expertise, and are backed either by local authorities or private swimming clubs. There are similar schemes in operation in most other countries.

Training schemes usually offer:

● the opportunity for large numbers of people to be involved in a structured programme of swimming training, suited to age, ability and ambition

● development programmes for elite swimmers, up to national and international standard

The schemes usually provide training at many levels, with each group having carefully-chosen performance goals. The amount of training increases progressively, from one hour per week for newcomers, up to the most elite groups who may train for twenty hours each week. Many of these elite swimmers achieve international selection, and go on to represent their country in the Commonwealth and Olympic Games.

Most large pools have a swimming club associated with them; joining the club and starting on their training scheme could be your first step on the ladder which leads to swimming success!

Badge schemes and survival awards

In Britain, there are numerous encouragement award schemes for swimmers young and old. These cover diving, synchro, water polo and survival as well as swimming. A number of organisations, including the Amateur Swimming Association (ASA), the English Schools Swimming Association (ESSA), the British Swimming Coaches Association (BSCA) and the British Lifesaving Association, and several sponsors, have cooperated to make this range possible. The list below gives brief details of the most popular schemes, and further information can be gained from the ASA, whose address is on page 46. Most other countries operate similar programmes, and we strongly recommend taking part in one or more of these schemes if at all possible.

ASA/ESSA Rainbow Award Scheme
For children of any age. Badges for 5-metre to 5,000-metre distance awards. No time limit.

ASA/ESSA Water Skills Award Scheme
Grades from one to six; starts with basic confidence and buoyancy skills and progresses to stroke technique. Some of the tasks have to be performed within a time limit.

ASA National Challenge Awards
Bronze, silver, gold and honours grades. Minimum recommended age: five years. Introduces a range of skills and encourages good ability in a variety of strokes and techniques. Includes some survival tasks which are swum in clothing.

ASA Personal Survival Awards
Levels one and two; a more advanced scheme concentrating on the theory and practice of survival skills.

ASA Swim Fit Awards
For children and adults. Designed to keep you swimming! Badges for distances from 10 miles to 1500 miles. The distances are cumulative, so that the first award, ten miles, also puts you halfway towards the twenty-mile one, and so on.

BCSA National Progressive Badge Award Scheme
A comprehensive scheme of badges for style, speed and distance.

9

Making more of swimming

Once you have learned the basic skills required to swim, you will discover a vast range of swimming and aquatic activities. Not everybody wants to race: you may be happy to continue with swimming purely for fun, for fitness, or as a social activity with friends. Maybe you fancy the rough-and-tumble of water polo, the grace of synchronised swimming, or the challenge of long-distance records. Let's have a look at some of the further sporting opportunities that are open to you now that you are a swimmer...

Water polo

Water polo is a great game, both for adults and for children, who take to it very easily. However, its development over the years has been restricted in many countries because of a basic shortage of pools. It is hard for teams to gain frequent access to pools which are in demand by other swimmers and divers. This is a pity, because youngsters usually develop a great enthusiasm for the game when they do get the chance to play it. If there is a water-polo club or group near you, do make contact and find out more. The game appears to have complex rules, but don't worry too much about these at first. Before you start playing properly, you will have to concentrate on these basic skills:

- Swimming with the ball
- Picking up the ball
- Throwing the ball
- Catching the ball

Throwing and catching need to be practised with one hand, so that your other arm can control your position. You can practise this with a few friends in any pool which allows balls to be taken into the water. The better you are at swimming, the better you will develop water-polo skills. Fitness is essential, and most of today's competitive water-polo players were initially competitive swimmers. When you start, you will no doubt be playing a simplified version of the game, with the rules adapted to suit your age-group and abilities. This will ensure close and exciting games which will be thoroughly enjoyable. However, always try to stick to these basics which you will have to obey when you progress to the "real" game:

- Play the ball with one hand only
- Keep your feet off the bottom
- No taking the ball under the water
- No pulling or sinking an opponent
- No holding the ball with both hands

In the full game of water polo, each team has seven players in the water, as well as four reserves on the pool-side. A match lasts for twenty minutes of actual playing time, divided into four five-minute quarters. The intervals between the quarters are of two minutes each, during which time the teams change ends.

Just as in football, the object is to score by getting the ball into your opponents' cage-like goal, while defending your own. The skills of dribbling and passing are very important, and you have to remember to touch the ball with one hand only. An exception to this rule is made for the goalkeepers, who may use both hands and are also allowed to punch it — something forbidden for all other players.

The teams wear caps of different colours for identification. The referee stands on the pool-side and signals with a whistle and a stick with a flag matching the the cap colours on each end.

Once these few rules have been observed, your ability will quickly develop with practice. Within a good club, individual and team players will enjoy the game and make rapid improvement.

As with all team games, a good coach is important, so you should look for a club where coaching is stressed.

Diving

Diving can be a fun part of the sport of swimming, and one which youngsters will be keen to take up once they can swim competently.

Left and above: *Alison Roffey, the ASA National Junior Springboard Champion, displays the grace and gymnastic agility of top-grade diving during a practice session at Leeds International Pool.*

However, diving can be dangerous if you do not stick to the safety rules. Here they are — *they must be observed at all times*:

- Only dive into safe, deep water, at the local pool where it says it is safe to dive. Never dive into canals, rivers or gravel pits where the depth is unknown.

- Never dive into water which is so deep that you would not be happy to swim in it.

- If you suffer from ear trouble or a cold, do not dive without first taking medical advice.

- Understand that diving is a *progressive* sport; only attempt dives for which you have trained and which you are confident of achieving successfully.

Mark Shipman completes a reverse dive from the springboard as Alison awaits her turn. The water jets make the surface more visible to the divers.

Beating fear

Fear may be a problem for anyone starting to dive, and can be a real obstacle for children. Often the fear of having your head underwater in a strange attitude is enough to put you off. The trick is to build up confidence gradually, just as when learning to do the breast stroke. Here is a simple progression which will make anyone a safe diver quite quickly:

1 Start off standing in shallow water and bobbing your face down into it. From there, it is a simple step to crouching down to touch your feet, then to picking up an object from the bottom of the pool.

2 Try some confidence exercises in deeper water: learn how to breathe out steadily as you rise up after having kept your head about a metre under the surface.

3 Once you are happy with this, try a few jumps into the deep water.

4 Now try some surface dives.

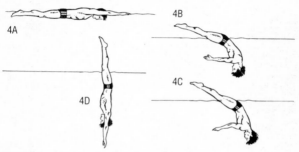

5 Sitting dives or rolls should not be a problem.

6 From sitting to kneeling is a small step — try some kneeling dives or rolls.

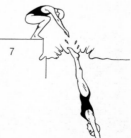

7 Now for the *crouch roll*...

8 ...and the *crouch dive*.

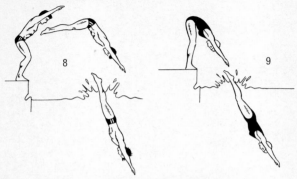

9 The *pike fall* is almost the real thing...

10 ... and the *spring header* is!

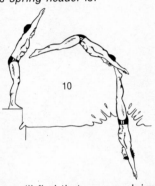

11 Finally, you will find that you are doing the the *plain header* and trying to get good style into it.

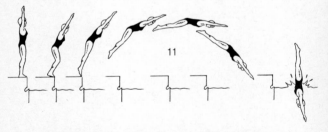

Once you can do a good plain header every time, entering the water vertically and without letting your legs flop around in the air, you are a diver. You have the basic technique which can be practised and improved until you are capable of competitive performance. You can't do this on your own — you must have a good coach or instructor, both to tell you what to do, and to tell you what you are doing wrong!

If you think that you would enjoy diving, the best advice we can give is to join a diving club as soon as possible. That way you will be assured of good coaching, and will be able to progress through the sport with the essential safety backup.

Synchronised swimming

Synchronised swimming, or *synchro* as it is familiarly known, has been one of the most rapidly developing areas of the sport in recent years.

Starting from small beginnings in the 1960s, synchro has evolved from its original concept of a slow, graceful water ballet, into a demanding new sport which is now a popular Olympic activity.

One of the great attractions of synchro is that you can participate even if you are a relative newcomer to swimming. It does not *have* to be performed competitively — you can enjoy taking part, or watching just for the entertainment value. Many young girls find that synchro is a more attractive option than competition race training. However, if you want to take part at the highest competitive level, you will find that the training is just as strenuous and demanding as for the top level of any other physical sport.

Synchro is similar to sports such as ice skating and gymnastics. The important elements are *figures* and *routines*. The *figures* are where certain combinations of movements are put together; as in ice skating, you need to be an expert to appreciate fully the level of skills required. The *routines* are very similar to the free-skating part of an ice programme; the swimmers wear attractive costumes and perform to music.

Competitive synchro can be performed solo, as a duet, or in teams of eight. The sport is becoming increasingly popular, and there are now many synchro clubs throughout the country. These vary considerably in standard, which is largely dependent on the quality of the coaches. If you are thinking of taking up synchro seriously, do check with a few clubs if at all possible, and pick the one that looks as if it will offer you the best opportunities for learning. Your local swimming pool or the ASA will be able to tell you which clubs there are in your area.

10

How the sport is run

In England, the sport of swimming is governed by the Amateur Swimming Association, which was formed in 1886. There are equivalent organisations in Scotland, Wales and Ireland. Over the years the ASA has steadily grown to its present size with nearly 1,700 clubs encompassing 300,000 swimmers. However, the sport is not confined to club members; it is also an extremely popular recreational activity with many millions of casual participants who swim regularly for fun and for fitness. Within the ASA there are separate branches dealing with competitive swimming, diving, synchro and water polo.

Today the ASA is part of a world-wide network of clubs and ruling bodies. The world governing body for swimming is called the *Fédération Internationale de Natation Amateur* (*FINA*). All premier swimming events, including the Olympic Games, are held under FINA laws.

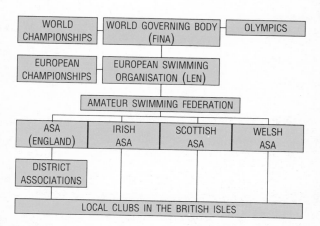

Figure 18 How competitive swimming in the British Isles fits into the world organisation; other countries have comparable structures

Useful addresses

British Isles

The Amateur Swimming Association
Harold Fern House
Derby Square
Loughborough
Leicestershire
LE11 0AL

Tel: 0509 230431

The English Schools Swimming Association
3 Maybank Grove
Liverpool
L17 6DW

Tel: 051-427 3707

The Royal Life Saving Society UK
Mountbatten House
Studley
Warwickshire
B80 7NN

Tel: 0527 853943

ASA/ESSA Awards
Miss L V Cook
12 Kings Avenue
Woodford Green
Essex
IG8 0JA

Tel: 01-504 9361

The Irish Amateur Swimming Association
6 Maywood Crescent
Dublin 5
Eire

Tel: 0001 601222

The Scottish Amateur Swimming Association
Airthrey Castle
University of Stirling
Stirling
FK9 4LA
Scotland

Tel: 0786 70544

The Welsh Amateur Swimming Association
National Sports Centre for Wales
Sophia Gardens
Cardiff
CF1 9SW
Wales

Tel: 0222 397571

Overseas

Australian Swimming Inc
PO Box 169
Kippax
ACT 2615
Australia

The Aquatic Federation of Canada
2180 Marine Drive
Suite 1607
Oakville
Ontario
Canada
L6L 5V2

The New Zealand Amateur Swimming Association
PO Box 11–115
Wellington
New Zealand

The Secretary
South Africa Amateur Swimming Union
PO Box 6355
Roggebaai 8012
Capetown
South Africa

International

Fédération Internationale de Natation Amateur
Honorary Secretary
Ross E Wales
425 Walnut
Suite 1610
Cincinnati
OH 45202
United States of America